| h | n | **P** | **O** |   |   |   |   |   |   |
|---|---|---|---|---|---|---|---|---|---|
| l | o | p | s |   |   |   |   |   |   |
| e | c | j | h | f | a | t | r | y | e | o |
| q | i | n | t | **C** | **H** | **A** | **N** | **G** | **E** | d | a |
| l | n | a | m | y | f | w | a | s | k | p | s |
| n | f | a | e | t | e | g | k | b | c | r | f |
| **B** | **R** | **E** | **A** | **K** | **T** | **H** | **R** | **O** | **U** | **G** | **H** |

MW01258077

| h | n | **P** | **O** | **W** | **E** | **R** | l | c | t | r | i |
|---|---|---|---|---|---|---|---|---|---|---|---|
| l | o | p | s | d | f | e | b | n | k | a | m |
| e | c | j | h | f | a | t | r | y | e | s | o |
| q | i | n | t | **C** | **H** | **A** | **N** | **G** | **E** | d | a |
| l | n | a | m | y | f | w | a | s | k | p | s |
| n | f | a | e | t | e | g | k | b | c | r | f |
| **B** | **R** | **E** | **A** | **K** | **T** | **H** | **R** | **O** | **U** | **G** | **H** |

*Praying Your Way*
*Through Difficult Times*
*A 30-Day Devotional*

# DR. CHERI FREY

gatekeeper press
Tampa, Florida

Power, Change, Breakthrough:
Praying Your Way Through Difficult Times

Published by Gatekeeper Press
7853 Gunn Hwy., Suite 209
Tampa, FL 33626
www.GatekeeperPress.com

Library of Congress Control Number: 2023940386

ISBN (paperback): 9781662941122
eISBN: 9781662941139

*I would like to*
*dedicate this book*

*to my loving husband, Brent,*
*my rock;*

*my sister, Danielle,*
*the wind beneath my wings;*

*and everyone who prayed for me*
*during this season.*

# Contents

Introduction                                           3

## SECTION ONE: **POWER**

1.  Teach Us to Pray                                  10
2.  He Is                                             14
3.  The Covenant                                      17
4.  Some Assembly Required                            21
5.  Express Yourself                                  25
6.  A Thorn                                           28
7.  Rough Seas                                        31
8.  Say the Word                                      34
9.  If                                                37
10. Keep on Praying                                   40

## SECTION TWO: **CHANGE**

11. Seasons Change                                    44
12. A Sure Foundation                                 47
13. Same God                                          50
14. Root of Bitterness                                53
15. Though He Slay Me                                 56

16. Strength to Endure                         59
17. Joy of Contentment                         62
18. It's in Your Praise                        65
19. Who You Say I Am                           68
20. Change of Heart                            71

SECTION THREE: BREAKTHROUGH

21. The Small Things                           76
22. Give Me My Mountain                        79
23. Wait for It                                82
24. Temporary Pain                             86
25. For My Good                                89
26. When God Says No                           92
27. Even If                                    95
28. Nevertheless                               98
29. It Is Finished                            101
30. Recommissioned                            105

Not the end...                                109

# Introduction

"Do you want children?" the doctor asked us.

We both replied yes.

"Good, you can have children. But they won't be your biological children."

He was speaking directly to me. Just minutes prior, the reproductive endocrinologist diagnosed me with primary ovarian insufficiency, or premature ovarian failure. In less fancy words, I was essentially postmenopausal at the age of thirty-four. Although he couldn't say for sure, based on my numbers, the doctor predicted this change occurred years ago. I had been on birth control for many years, so I was unaware of what was happening. When I stopped my birth control pills six months prior to my annual appointment with my gynecologist in 2019, I had no idea that it would be the last time I felt normal. Months of no menstrual cycle coupled with night sweats and insomnia followed. After a few blood tests, here I was. Diagnosis: infertile. Devastation does not even begin to describe what I felt. It was what, I imagine, suffocating must feel like: excruciating pain coursing through my body, while trying desperately to cling to life. I felt helpless, and even though I was in the room with two doctors, my husband, and one of my best friends, I still felt alone.

"Either you have a stellar poker face or you are taking this very well," the doctor said.

I conjured up a brief smile. I did have a stellar poker face. Up to that point, life had taught me that very rarely does it benefit me to show emotion, so I picked a place on his face to stare while he went through our options for starting a family. I thought about so much in the remaining fifteen minutes we spent with him. I thought about the day I met my husband. I thought about falling in love with him and how good that had felt. I thought about the day he proposed to me. I thought about our wedding day and our wedding night. I thought about all the plans I had made for us—all the baby names I picked out to match my new last name. I thought about all the babies I had helped to usher into the world as a medical student and as a friend.

I tuned in and out as the discussion went on. The doctor told us that because I had no eggs left, IVF was not an option. We could decide between donor eggs, donor embryos, and adoption. We finished the appointment by discussing the additional tests I would need. More blood tests, to check things like my chromosomes, and a DEXA scan to check the strength of my bones. Because I entered menopause so early, I was at risk of other medical issues, like osteoporosis. We finished up with his nurse, who walked us through some additional paperwork, and then we were off to process our new normal.

As we sat at home that night, I finally let out some tears. My husband held me but said very little. My mind was racing with terrible thoughts. Does he still love me? Am I still beautiful to him? Does he regret marrying me? At this point, we had been married for only a year and a half. I thought more than once that maybe it was better for him to just divorce me and start over. I was sad for myself, but I felt even worse for placing this burden on him.

If it were possible, I would have stayed in bed for the rest of the year. Instead, I got up each morning, cried my eyes out on my drive to work, then drowned myself in work. Work was my only escape. I could focus on something else, and for eight hours, forget about my own problems. I did pretty well until a few months later when I got a call from the radiologist. She had the results of my DEXA scan, and they were so bad that she had to call to confirm my demographics.

"And you are how old?" She asked. I answered thirty four. "I see," she replied.

She sent me the results that showed I had pretty significant osteoporosis in my spine and hip. I would have to see yet another specialist. I told my office manager that I needed a minute. I locked myself in my office and cried like a baby over my lunch break. *Why? Why God? I'm thirty-four years old with the body of an eighty-year-old. How could this happen to me? Why would this happen to me? Not that anyone deserves this, but God, I walk with you. I talk with you. God I trust you.*

I reached a breaking point. It wasn't just that the doctor said I could never have children. It was looking in the mirror and not seeing the woman I used to see. I didn't recognize myself. It was the thought of being on medication, being at risk for breast cancer and early dementia. It was the mood swings and hot flashes, thinning hair and dry skin. It felt like life had been sucked right out of me just when I was starting to live. After four years of medical school and four years of residency, I was finally living my dream, and now this. It felt unfair.

Those close to me tried their best to encourage me. They prayed for me and with me. They reminded me of God's promises. They remained optimistic and hopeful, but more often than not, I resented their words of encouragement. Soon, I began to resent God. I didn't want to pray. I didn't want to worship. My quiet time went to nap time. Sure, I showed up to church, but I wasn't *present*. I didn't want to preach and I didn't want to teach. Occasionally I would feel obliged to, so I would put something together just to keep those around me in the dark about just how badly I was doing. I was bitter. I was sinking and I didn't see a way out. Every time someone asked me about having kids, I sank further and further into the dark place. As you can imagine, as a thirty-something-year-old married woman, I got asked a lot. As time went on, I grew more bitter with God.

After a year passed, I heard the Lord for the first time in a long time. It was a gentle yet firm voice. He said, "What was it all for?" Confused, I started to think, *What was WHAT all for?* He said, "All that *church*." Wow! I felt so convicted. See, I was "raised" in the church, and for as long as I can remember, I have been a believer. I don't remember my life without Christ. I come from a long line of pastors and ministers. I, fortunately, never had to "come to Jesus." He was always right there. I preached my first sermon at the age of nine. Certainly, I had my wayward years; I am far from perfect. But I never had any doubts about my faith until now. I knew scripture and taught many lessons on trusting God, waiting on God, believing God. Yet when it was time to put my faith to work, it was...dead? God had to call me out. What good was all the scripture memorization, the ministry, and the lessons if I couldn't activate my faith when it counted most?

I still had no intention of breaking up with my new companion, grief, until one day I was scrolling Facebook. You've probably seen those posts with hidden words and a caption that reads, "The first three words you see will be the theme of the next year." I usually scroll past those, but for some reason, I stopped. I glanced and saw three words: Power, Change, Breakthrough. I repeated them. Power, Change, Breakthrough. I kept saying them over and over, and they began to resonate with me. Power, Change, Breakthrough. I wrote them down and began to meditate on them every day.

I began to feel a desire to seek the Lord. I asked God to open up my understanding. What did Power, Change, Breakthrough mean, and how could I apply it to my situation? The Spirit began to speak to me. He revealed that I was bitter because I wanted God to fix my circumstances, when all along, God wanted to use my circumstances to fix me.

If you are reading this book, I'm guessing you also need a Breakthrough. It doesn't matter so much *what* you're going through. For me it was infertility, but yours may be a broken relationship, sickness, death of a loved one, depression, or financial hardship. The circumstance does not matter because the word of God says, "Many are the afflictions of the righteous: but the Lord delivereth him out of them all" (Psalm 34:19 King James Version [KJV]). Whatever you are experiencing, God can and will deliver you. Your breakthrough may not happen overnight. It didn't happen overnight for me. So if you want a "get blessed quick" scheme, you are reading the wrong book. This book is about renewing our minds, softening our hearts, and walking out our faith no matter what life has thrown at us. It's about approaching our trials with a new outlook. *Power, Change,*

*Breakthrough.* It is the *Power* of God that *Changes* us, and when we have been changed, then and only then can we receive our *Breakthrough.*

As you journey with me over the next thirty days, my prayer for you is that God will radically reveal Himself to you in new ways. As you invite Him into your heart, you will feel His presence and experience the fullness of joy, even during your most difficult times.

## Section One

# POWER

"But you shall receive power when the Holy Spirit has come upon you; and you shall be [a]witnesses to Me in Jerusalem, and in all Judea and Samaria, and to the end of the earth." (Acts 1:8 New King James Version [NKJV])

# Day 1

## *Teach Us to Pray*

"Now Jesus was praying in a certain place, and when he finished, one of his disciples said to him, 'Lord, teach us to pray, as John taught his disciples.'" (Luke 11:1 English Standard Version [ESV])

During my second year in residency, I was reading the book of Luke when I came across this verse. Although I'd read this passage many times, I felt motivated to dive deeper. What prompted the disciples to ask Jesus for this lesson on prayer? The disciples were intimately acquainted with Jesus. They saw Him perform many miracles and teach sermons. They saw firsthand how Jesus's teachings drew crowds and changed lives. However, they did not ask Jesus to teach them to preach and they did not say, "Lord, teach us to heal the sick." The disciples asked Jesus to teach them to pray. Could it be that after spending so much time with Jesus, they recognized how important prayer was to him and how devoted to prayer Jesus was? He rose early in the morning to pray, and likely never said any word, did anything, or went anywhere without praying first. The disciples probably concluded that it was his prayer life that was the true source of his power.

When I suffered through the grief of my diagnosis, I could barely find the words to pray. Many times, I thought to myself, *is God even listening?* It felt like prayer was a waste of time because my circumstances didn't change. If God wanted to do something, He could just do it. He didn't need my prayers. But prayer isn't a suggestion. Pray is a directive. Ephesians 6:18 says, "And pray in the Spirit on all occasions with all kinds of prayers and requests."

Prayer is how we stay connected to God. When we cut off our prayer life, we cut off the source of our power. When things get tough, the enemy wants us to abandon our prayer life because he knows how valuable it is. He will try to convince you your prayers are not being heard. He will try to distract you or disrupt your prayer time. You must set aside dedicated time to pray each day. The more you have going on, the more you need to pray. There should be no such excuse as "too busy to pray." St. Francis de Sales said, "Every one of us needs half an hour of prayer every day, except when we are busy—then we need an hour." Our goal should be not to settle for a *prayer life*, but to have a *life of prayer*.

When we face a storm, we need prayer even more. However, prayer should not be our 911, but our 411; meaning, prayer should not be something we dial up in case of an emergency. Prayer should be our source of information. Prayer is where we get a glimpse of God's plan. So if we want to be connected to the Operator of the Universe, we must pray. We must make prayer as natural to us as breathing. Pray publicly, privately, in human tongues, and in the heavenly languages. Prayer reaches places you cannot touch or see. It is the *prayer* of the righteous that availeth much (James 5:16 KJV). The Bible says not to be anxious for anything, but by *prayer* and supplication, make our requests known (Philippians 4:6 ESV).

If anyone is sick, let the elders *pray* over him (James 5:14 ESV). When things are hard, God calls us to pray.

As a response to the disciples' request, Jesus answered them with what is known as the Lord's Prayer. You do not have to use this exact prayer. You can use the Lord's Prayer as a model for your own personal prayers. There are various models for those who struggle with knowing *how* to pray, such as ACTS, which stands for Adoration/Acknowledgment, Confession, Thanksgiving, Supplication. It is not as important to use a model as it is to be reverent, sincere, and consistent.

If you need a job, pray. If your loved one is sick, pray. If your debt is piling up, pray. If you are going through a divorce, pray. If your child ran away from home, pray. If your coworkers are working your last nerve like it's their part-time job, pray.

Meditation: "Is anyone among you in trouble? Let them pray." (James 5:13 New International Version [NIV])

Your journey toward your *breakthrough* starts with power. In order to receive power, you need prayer. Recommit yourself to praying by writing out a prayer on the pages to follow.

# Day 2

# *He Is*

"Moses said to God, 'Suppose I go to the Israelites and say to them, 'The God of your fathers has sent me to you,' and they ask me, 'What is his name?' Then what shall I tell them?' God said to Moses, 'I am who I am. This is what you are to say to the Israelites: "I am has sent me to you."'" (Exodus 3:13–14 NIV)

In Exodus, God calls Moses from a burning bush and instructs him to go to Egypt and deliver the Israelites from slavery. When Moses asks who he should say sent him, God replies I AM. We might think this was an error in translation or a sly remark, but God was purposefully revealing to Moses, and to us, something new about His nature.

God often reveals Himself to His people through His attributes. He appeared to Abraham in Gen 17:1 as El-Shaddai, the Almighty God. He again appeared as the Everlasting God in Gen 21:33. God further revealed Himself by taking the names Raphe, meaning healer (Exodus 15:2); Shalom, meaning peace (Judges 6:24); and Tsidkenu, meaning righteousness (Jeremiah 23:6). Giving Himself the name I AM was God once again revealing Himself through His attributes.

The Hebrew translation for "I AM that I am" is "Ehyeh Asher Ehyeh." It means "to be." This verb conveys two tenses: one for actions that have been completed and one for actions that have yet to be completed. It's as if God was saying to Moses, I am that I am and I will become who I choose to become. When God says "I AM that I AM," He is reminding His people that He is what we need for today and what we need for what is to come. God's character doesn't change, but instead, He reveals Himself in different ways at different times in our lives. He is the only one who can supply all our needs. Because of this, you don't need a different god for sun, rain, healing, protection, or fertility. God IS and will be everything we will ever need. A healer? He IS. A deliverer? He IS. A provider? He IS.

Meditation: "But my God shall supply all your needs according to His riches in glory by Christ Jesus." (Phil 4:19 NKJV)

God has the *power* to meet your every need. Write down what you need God to be in this season.

..............................................................................
..............................................................................
..............................................................................
..............................................................................
..............................................................................
..............................................................................
..............................................................................
..............................................................................
..............................................................................
..............................................................................
..............................................................................
..............................................................................
..............................................................................
..............................................................................
..............................................................................
..............................................................................
..............................................................................
..............................................................................

# Day 3
---

# *The Covenant*

"The Lord had said to Abram, 'Go from your country, your people and your father's household to the land I will show you. I will make you into a great nation, and I will bless you; I will make your name great, and you will be a blessing. I will bless those who bless you, and whoever curses you I will curse; and all peoples on earth will be blessed through you.'" (Genesis 12:1–3 NIV)

Abraham is known as the father of many nations. He is one of the most well-known patriarchs of God's chosen people, the Israelites. In Genesis 12, God made a covenant with Abram, later known as Abraham. God promises Abram He would make him a "great nation." God promises Abram land, descendants, and prosperity. At that time, when two people entered into a covenant, they were each agreeing to be responsible for their portion. In order to "seal" the covenant, animals were torn in two pieces and the two parties agreeing to the covenant would walk between the torn animals. This was done to signify that if either party broke the covenant, they would meet the same fate as these animals. God's covenant with Abram was different. In Chapter 15 of Genesis, God places the burden of fulfilling the covenant solely on Himself as He passes between animals while Abram is asleep. After God confirmed His covenant, He warned Abram that the Israelites would endure some suffering, but ultimately His promises would be fulfilled and they would inherit all that He swore to Abram that day.

Centuries later, when the Israelites found themselves in slavery and facing genocide at the hands of the Egyptians, they cried out to God. The Bible says God heard them and remembered His covenant with Abram, Isaac, and Jacob. Therefore, when the Israelites turned to God, He was compelled to intervene.

The year following my diagnosis was extremely tough. I didn't share the news with many people, including some of my best friends. I mostly carried the sorrow alone. I rarely expressed my pain to God Himself. I felt completely powerless in my situation until I remembered God made a covenant with me too. Unlike the sacrificial animals used for the covenant with Abram, God chose to send His son Jesus Christ as the ultimate sacrifice. God promised those who believe in His son that they would have everlasting life. Just as Isaiah prophesied that Jesus would bear our transgressions, he also prophesied that Jesus would bear our griefs and sorrows and "by His stripes we would be healed" (Isaiah 53:4–5 NKJV). I realized the pain of my infertility was not mine to carry, so I unburdened myself and placed my diagnosis firmly in God's capable hands.

When we find ourselves bearing griefs and sorrows we were never meant to bear, we must remind God of His covenant with us just as the Israelites did. Let us not simply complain about our situation. Instead, cry out to God and remind Him of His word and His covenant with us. God has the power to change our situations just like He did for the Israelites. Prayer gives God permission to intervene in our lives. When we call on Him, He will respond.

Meditation: "Call to Me, and I will answer you, and show you great and mighty things, which you do not know." (Jeremiah 33:3 NKJV)

Write down whatever is burdening you at the moment. Does it seem like an unbearable weight? You could be shouldering a burden you were never meant to carry and certainly were never meant to carry alone. Cry out to God and give Him permission to intervene. Allow His *power* to sustain you.

...........................................................................................................

...........................................................................................................

...........................................................................................................

...........................................................................................................

...........................................................................................................

...........................................................................................................

...........................................................................................................

...........................................................................................................

...........................................................................................................

...........................................................................................................

...........................................................................................................

...........................................................................................................

...........................................................................................................

...........................................................................................................

...........................................................................................................

...........................................................................................................

...........................................................................................................

...........................................................................................................

...........................................................................................................

# Day 4

## *Some Assembly Required*

"For the Lord your God is the one who goes with you to fight for you against your enemies to give you victory." (Deuteronomy 20:4 NIV)

Imagine what the Israelite spies felt as they first laid eyes on the promised land. It was beautiful, fertile, pleasing to the eye, and...filled with giants. Their promised land, Canaan, was already occupied, and Hebron, an exceptional city, was extremely well fortified. The walk back to camp must have felt particularly long for ten of the twelve spies. Perhaps the Israelites assumed that their promised land was somewhere completely uninhabited, just waiting for them to walk in and settle down. Did they picture it would come just as easily as the manna fell from heaven? Or that God would clear the path the same way He parted the Red Sea? Judging by their reactions to the spies' report, I'm guessing they weren't expecting to have to work for it. Discouraged and uninspired, ten of the spies gave the most horrible report to Moses.

Forget about it, they said. There's no way we are getting in there. Only two of the spies had the audacity to say it was possible. Joshua and Caleb, despite what they saw physically, saw something even greater with their spiritual eyes and they would not be dissuaded simply because it would require effort.

I think back on my own life. I was halfway through year three of a four-year college scholarship, when God called me to do a 180 and go into medicine. Up until that point in college, I had taken only one science class and it was a psychology course. *There's no way I can do this*, I thought to myself. I started adding up all the classes I would need to take: biology, chemistry, physics, not to mention the standardized admission test. These were ten-foot giants to someone who was a year away from graduating with a degree in advertising. But these giants were standing between me and my promised land. There was no way around them, I would have to go through them. I thought about throwing in the towel, until God placed some Joshuas and Calebs in my path. It certainly wasn't easy, but God took what I did and made it more than enough. I give God all the glory for bringing me to where I am today, but it wasn't without hard work and sacrifice.

Sometimes, we expect when God blesses us or promises something to us, that it won't require anything on our part. Yes, sometimes our blessings are ready-to-go, like manna falling from heaven. But sometimes they come in pieces with instructions stating "assembly required," like a promised land filled with giants. Don't be discouraged by the work, the process, or the challenges. God will equip you with the *power* to overcome every giant in your path.

Meditation: "Yet in all these things we are more than conquerors through Him who loved us." (Romans 8:37 NKJV)

Just as God was with the Israelites as they fought to take possession of their promised land, He will enable you and see you through your own battles. Ask yourself what giants are standing in the way of your promised land and ask God for the supernatural *power* to conquer them.

# Day 5

# *Express Yourself*

"My tears have been my food day and night, while men say to me all day long, 'Where is your God?'" (Psalms 42:3 NKJV)

The Bible describes David as a man after God's own heart. While many people debate what exactly that term means, most will agree that David had a special relationship with God. He was chosen from among his brothers to be the next king of Israel. He had an audience with King Saul and was given Saul's daughter, Princess Michal, in marriage. David slew the Philistine giant Goliath and won many battles. Although David was blessed by God, he also struggled with his own sins and endured many hardships. He was an adulterer and a murderer. David lost a child, was a refugee, and his own son tried to overthrow him. Through these hardships, David penned some of the most desperate and passionate psalms. Psalm 22 was written as David hid in a cave to avoid his capture and death.

"My God, my God, why have you forsaken me? Why are you so far from saving me, from the words of my groaning? O my God, I cry by day, but you do not answer, and by night, but I find no rest." (Psalm 22:1–2 NIV)

Pain and suffering have a way of making you feel alone, even when you are surrounded by others. It can be difficult to feel the presence of God in dark places. Sometimes we feel abandoned by God. This is certainly what David was feeling and something I've experienced as well. As much as I wanted to talk about my feelings, for a long time I could not bring myself to do it. I couldn't even write about it in a journal. Our difficulties are not meant to separate us from God. They are an opportunity to draw us closer to Him, but if we are not careful, they can have the opposite effect. David fought this by constantly expressing himself to God. He poured out his heart through the psalms. We should do the same. Little by little, I opened myself up to God. Honestly, I didn't have nice things to say at first. But it's ok to tell God how we feel, while maintaining reverence. Express to Him anger, pain, disappointment. God is big enough to handle our emotions.

We all know what happens to a relationship when there are uncommunicated feelings. It begins to break down. Your relationship with God is no different. God desires an intimate relationship with you. Intimacy suffers when we are not radically honest. Talk to God regularly in prayer and through journaling. God is waiting for you to talk to Him. More importantly, He wants to talk back.

Meditation: "On the day I called, You answered me; You made me bold with strength in my soul." (Psalm 138:3 NKJV)

The psalmist received a dose of God's *power* when he cried out to Him. Tell God how you feel. Write your own psalm, sincerely expressing yourself to Him.

# SECTION ONE: POWER

..........................................................................................................
..........................................................................................................
..........................................................................................................
..........................................................................................................
..........................................................................................................
..........................................................................................................
..........................................................................................................
..........................................................................................................
..........................................................................................................
..........................................................................................................
..........................................................................................................
..........................................................................................................
..........................................................................................................
..........................................................................................................
..........................................................................................................
..........................................................................................................
..........................................................................................................
..........................................................................................................
..........................................................................................................
..........................................................................................................

# Day 6

# *A Thorn*

"So to keep me from becoming conceited because of the surpassing greatness of the revelations, a thorn was given me in the flesh, a messenger of Satan to harass me, to keep me from becoming conceited." (2 Corinthians 12:7 ESV)

Paul was an apostle, a true servant who spent his ministry building churches, making disciples, and preaching the gospel. Yet, the Bible says a thorn was given to him. You read that correctly. It was given to him. God allowed it. God permitted it. Although the Bible doesn't specify what kind of problem Paul had, we do know it was something painful and agonizing. The Bible says, three times Paul asked God to take it away. God's response to Paul, "My grace is sufficient for you" (2 Corinthians 12:9 ESV).

What happens when the prayers seemingly go answered? When the prognosis doesn't improve or when our loved one dies despite our deepest cries for healing? How do we reconcile a great God with the weight of our pain and grief? Is God still good? And if so, why do so many suffer? I felt just like Paul as I pleaded with God to heal my body. His response: My grace is sufficient for you.

What exactly does His grace enable us to do? Grace, simply put, is getting something you don't deserve. When God says "my grace is sufficient," He is telling us that He will give us the power to minister through this. His grace will sustain us so that our ailments, our circumstances, our doubters, our enemies will not hinder us or His purpose for our lives. His grace will carry us such that when people discover what we've been dealing with, they will be shocked and say, "I don't know how you are able to do what you do, while dealing with what you are dealing with." Our response will be, "It's only by the grace of God."

God will even use our thorns as a basis for our ministry. It is often in the most painful parts of our lives that our ministries are born. Take this book, for example. Would I be writing this book if I had not gone through my own trial? Probably not.

God also gave Paul a thorn to keep him humble. "To keep me from being conceited," Paul says (2 Corinthians 12:7 ESV). In other words, so I don't become prideful and take all the credit. I have this thorn as a reminder that it was by the grace of God and nothing else, that I am what I am. This is why in the end, Paul can rejoice in his suffering. Paul understood that his human weakness was an opportunity to demonstrate the *power* of God at work in his life. Instead of praying our thorns away, we need to recognize how God may be using them to keep us near to Him and the path He has laid out for us.

Meditation: "But by the grace of God I am what I am, and His grace toward me was not in vain; but I labored more abundantly than they all, yet not I, but the grace of God *which* was with me." (1 Corinthians 15:10 NKJV)

Ask God to fortify you with His grace to endure the path He has laid out for you.

# Day 7

## *Rough Seas*

"And the same day, when the evening was come, he saith unto them, Let us pass over unto the other side. And when they had sent away the multitude, they took him even as he was in the ship. And there were also with him other little ships. And there arose a great storm of wind, and the waves beat into the ship, so that it was now full. And he was in the hinder part of the ship, asleep on a pillow: and they awake him, and say unto him, Master, carest thou not that we perish?" (Mark 4:35–38 KJV)

In this text, Jesus instructs his disciples to join him in the boat and cross the sea. Jesus certainly knew there was a storm coming. In fact, the sea of Galilee was known for its sudden violent storms. Still, Jesus instructed the disciples to leave the safety of the shore and cross the sea where a storm would later arise.

Who would get in a boat, knowing a storm was coming? Most rational humans avoid storms at all costs. (An exception would be the meteorologists and storm chasers.) Yet, here we find Jesus's disciples in a very uncomfortable circumstance, having been led by Jesus into a storm. And what a storm it must have been. These experienced fishermen were so rattled by the storm, they thought they might die. They searched for Jesus only to find him... sleeping? How dare you be asleep right now, Jesus? You brought us out here. Now here we are facing a terrible storm, and you're sleeping!

Maybe, just maybe, we can reconcile a God that would allow us to go through a storm, but what about a God that leads you into a storm? That doesn't seem right. The truth is, for believers, God often uses storms to reveal to us more of His character. Sure, we can read about His character, but a deeper understanding arises when you experience His character for yourself. With each experience, you learn to trust Him more. The disciples learned that Jesus's authority was not limited to wine and bread. The disciples saw firsthand that Jesus had the *power* to control even the wind and seas. Jesus was able to rest in the storm because he knew the power that lived inside of him. Through the Holy Spirit, we have access to that same power.

Meditation: "And Jesus came and spoke to them, saying, 'All authority has been given to Me in heaven and on earth.'" (Matthew 28:18 NKJV)

Storms will rise in our lives, sometimes without warning. We can be fully assured that God has everything under control, His control. Write a prayer and ask God for inner peace during your storm. Then begin to speak peace *to* your storm.

...................................................................................................

...................................................................................................

...................................................................................................

...................................................................................................

...................................................................................................

...................................................................................................

...................................................................................................

...................................................................................................

...................................................................................................

...................................................................................................

...................................................................................................

...................................................................................................

...................................................................................................

...................................................................................................

...................................................................................................

...................................................................................................

...................................................................................................

...................................................................................................

...................................................................................................

...................................................................................................

# Day 8

## *Say the Word*

"Now when Jesus had entered Capernaum, a centurion came to Him, pleading with Him, saying, 'Lord, my servant is lying at home paralyzed, dreadfully tormented.' And Jesus said to him, "I will come and heal him.' The centurion answered and said, 'Lord, I am not worthy that You should come under my roof. But only speak a word, and my servant will be healed.'" (Matthew 8:5–8 NKJV)

In Genesis Chapter 1, God created the heavens and the earth, and He did so by speaking it into existence. The Bible tells us, "And God said, 'Let there be light,' and there was light (Genesis 1:3 ESV). When God created man, He gave that same power to us on earth. "Let Us make man in Our image, according to Our likeness; let them have dominion over the fish of the sea, over the birds of the air, and over the cattle, over all the earth and over every creeping thing that creeps on the earth" (Genesis 1:26 NKJV). Then in Chapter 2, the Bible tells us, "Out of the ground the Lord God formed every beast of the field and every bird of the air, and brought them to Adam to see what he would call them. And whatever Adam called each living creature, that was its name" (Genesis 2:19 NKJV). God gave man dominion over the earth, and the way we exercise that dominion is with our speech. No other animals were given the ability to speak because there is power in our words. Proverbs 18:21 (NKJV) tells us, "Death and life are in the power of the tongue." Just as God spoke light into darkness, and Jesus spoke healing to the sick, our words have a way of bringing things into existence. When we understand the power that our words carry, we will use them wisely.

Then Jesus said to the centurion, "Go your way; and as you have believed, so let it be done for you." And his servant was healed that same hour. (Matthew 8:13 NKJV). The centurion understood the *power* of words. When we combine words with faith, nothing will be impossible.

Meditation: "For assuredly, I say to you, whoever says to this mountain, 'Be removed and be cast into the sea,' and does not doubt in his heart, but believes that those things he says will be done, he will have whatever he says." (Mark 11:23 NKJV)

It is simply not enough to think in your heart. If you want to see mountains move, you must say the words. Speak life, speak healing, speak provision, speak blessings. Use the pages to write out your declaration, then speak it out loud.

# Day 9

## *If*

"So when Jesus came, He found that he had already been in the tomb four days. Now Bethany was near Jerusalem, about two miles away. And many of the Jews had joined the women around Martha and Mary, to comfort them concerning their brother. Then Martha, as soon as she heard that Jesus was coming, went and met Him, but Mary was sitting in the house. Now Martha said to Jesus, 'Lord, if You had been here, my brother would not have died.'" (John 11:17–21 NKJV)

This is the narrative of Lazarus, the brother of Martha and Mary. The Bible states that Jesus loved Lazarus. We know that Jesus loved everyone, so the fact that the Bible goes out of the way to describe how Jesus felt about Lazarus and his sisters likely means that Jesus shared a special connection with them. They were his friends. So when Martha sends word that her brother is sick, I am sure she expected Jesus to drop everything and come to his rescue. This is not what Jesus did. The Bible says when he heard Lazarus was sick, Jesus stayed where he was two more days before traveling to Bethany. By the time he reached them, Lazarus had been buried four days (John 11:17). When Martha and Mary see Jesus, they express their disappointment. If only you were here, this terrible thing would not have happened. You, Lord, could have prevented this.

In the midst of my trials, I felt similar pain. I felt like God could have prevented this. I felt like God didn't show up for me when I needed Him. As a believer, there is a cognitive dissonance you experience when you face difficulty. I struggled knowing that God was ABLE to do anything, to keep me from anything, but yet He CHOSE to allow this to happen. As a child of God, you may be experiencing similar feelings during your trial. Have you thought, "If you love me God, why would you let this happen?"

Thankfully, Lazarus's story did not end in a tomb. Although Martha, Mary, and even Jesus had to endure the pain of losing Lazarus, God used this situation to demonstrate His power in ways they had not yet seen. Perhaps God wants to reveal Himself in new ways to you. He desires to take you from faith to faith (Romans 1:17). In order for God to grow you, you must believe that His power has no end. No matter how hopeless it seems, absolutely nothing is impossible to God. He has the *power* to do anything.

Meditation: "Jesus looked at them and said, 'With man this is impossible, but with God all things are possible.'" (Matthew 19:26 NIV)

What situations have you given up on? Where have you lost hope? Remember, God has the *power* to do anything.

# Day 10

## *Keep on Praying*

"On the twenty-fourth day of the first month, as I was standing on the bank of the great river (that is, the Tigris). I lifted up my eyes and looked, and behold, a man clothed in linen, with a belt of fine gold from Uphaz around his waist. His body was like beryl, his face like the appearance of lightning, his eyes like flaming torches, his arms and legs like the gleam of burnished bronze, and the sound of his words like the sound of a multitude....Then he said to me, 'Fear not, Daniel, for from the first day that you set your heart to understand and humbled yourself before your God, your words have been heard, and I have come because of your words. The prince of the kingdom of Persia withstood me twenty-one days, but Michael, one of the chief princes, came to help me, for I was left there with the kings of Persia.'" (Daniel 10:4–6,12–14 ESV)

In this text we learn that Daniel was in mourning over the persecution of his people, the Israelites. Daniel prayed and fasted for three weeks before he saw an angelic being carrying a message from God. The angelic being tells Daniel that God heard his very first prayer and sent a response right away, but the answer to Daniel's prayer could not reach him because there was a force opposing him. This demonic force he called the "prince of the kingdom of Persia." In order to reach Daniel, the angelic being had to call for backup.

In the midst of our trials, we may feel like God is not answering our prayers. However, there are times when God has indeed sent His response, but our adversary, the devil, is working against us to prevent us from receiving what God has for us. We have to remain cognizant that we "wrestle not against flesh and blood, but against principalities, against powers, against the rulers of the darkness of this world, against spiritual wickedness in high places" (Ephesians 6:12 KJV). There are spiritual forces working against us. Because Daniel continued to pray, God sent more angels to fight on Daniel's behalf.

Remember, we are not pestering God. Our consistent prayers may be the key to unlocking more of God's *power*. Keep on praying.

Meditation: "The insistent prayer of a righteous person is powerfully effective." (James 5:16 WEB)

Write out a prayer for a situation for which you are still waiting for an answer. Commit to praying it daily for the next twenty-one days.

## Section 2

# CHANGE

"Do not be shaped by this world; instead be changed within by a new way of thinking. Then you will be able to decide what God wants for you; you will know what is good and pleasing to him and what is perfect." (Romans 12:2 New Century Version [NCV])

# Day 11

# *Seasons Change*

"To everything there is a season, A time for every purpose under heaven: A time to be born, And a time to die; A time to plant, And a time to pluck what is planted; A time to kill, And a time to heal; A time to break down, And a time to build up; A time to weep, And a time to laugh; A time to mourn, And a time to dance; A time to cast away stones, And a time to gather stones; A time to embrace, And a time to refrain from embracing; A time to gain, And a time to lose; A time to keep, And a time to throw away; A time to tear, And a time to sew; A time to keep silence, And a time to speak; A time to love, And a time to hate; A time of war, And a time of peace." (Ecclesiastes 3:1–8 NKJV)

Since the beginning of time, the earth has operated on a schedule. The earth spins on its axis, creating night and day. We don't go to bed at night only *hoping* the sun rises in the morning. We expect nothing less. Around the sun the earth spins, creating fall, winter, spring, and summer. We know each season by the signs. For example, when the leaves turn orange and brown, we know fall is coming. The seasons may look different depending on where you live. Winter lasts a little longer up north. Heavy rains pour during hurricane season down south. We don't question it. We just prepare for it and ride it out.

Yet, when we think of our lives, we hardly ever consider the season. If we are not mindful, we may become frustrated that there is no harvest, when it is actually planting season. No matter where we are currently, we have an assurance that winter doesn't last forever. We have to apply this same philosophy when we enter undesirable seasons in our lives. *Will it always be like this?* is a thought I remember having constantly. I just couldn't imagine better days at first, no matter how hard I tried. But the truth is, better days *are* ahead. There are warm, sunny days in your future. We don't throw away our bathing suits because it's winter. We simply wait for summer. Have the same faith in God. Your season is coming.

Meditation: "At the right time, I, the LORD, will make it happen." (Isaiah 60:22)

*Change* your mind about how you view your present circumstances. Take some time to assess what season you are in right now.

....................................................................................................

....................................................................................................

....................................................................................................

....................................................................................................

....................................................................................................

....................................................................................................

....................................................................................................

....................................................................................................

....................................................................................................

....................................................................................................

....................................................................................................

....................................................................................................

....................................................................................................

....................................................................................................

....................................................................................................

....................................................................................................

....................................................................................................

....................................................................................................

....................................................................................................

....................................................................................................

# Day 12

## A Sure Foundation

"Everyone then who hears these words of mine and does them will be like a wise man who built his house on the rock. And the rain fell, and the floods came, and the winds blew and beat on that house, but it did not fall, because it had been founded on the rock." (Matthew 7:24–25 ESV)

Much like the weather, we have little control over the storms in our lives. What is within our control is our response to the storm. Our response to storms can be more revealing than anything else. I wish I could tell you that when presented with the diagnosis of early menopause, I stood up to it with complete faith and boldness, but that wouldn't be true. I crumbled. I professed faith, but when the storm came, I lost my mind. If you would have asked me years before my diagnosis how I would respond, I would have never guessed that I would have fallen so far off track.

The truth is, most of us do not know who we really are until we are pushed, pressed, or stretched. It's only in tough times that we can see the areas in our lives where our foundation is unsure. Storms can be mirrors for us, allowing us to see areas where we don't have as much faith as we thought. I learned a lot about myself through my storm. I learned where the holes in my faith were. I learned that I sometimes give up too easily. I learned that I was full of pride. I learned what I really valued in my life. I learned how far from perfect I was.

God desires to shape us into His image and bring us to an expected end. He wants to complete the work He started in us. Sometimes He works through the challenges we face. God will do whatever He has to do in order to transform us. When the work is complete, we will be like Jesus, who did not freak out in the storm, but instead rested.

The perfecting and the pruning is not comfortable, but it is necessary. Remember the saying "a smooth sea, never made a skilled sailor." Understand that even storms are an opportunity for growth, if we allow the Holy Spirit to work in us. Instead of focusing on the outward circumstance (the storm), it's time to focus on the inward (yourself). Then, as we grow, so will our response to storms.

Meditation: "My brethren, count it all joy when you fall into various trials, knowing that the testing of your faith produces patience. But let patience have its perfect work, that you may be perfect and complete, lacking nothing." (James 1:2–4 NKJV)

What is your current storm revealing about you?

# SECTION TWO: CHANGE

# Day 13

# *Same God*

"Jesus Christ *is* the same yesterday, today, and forever." (Hebrew 13:8 NKJV)

For years following my diagnosis, I had no hunger or thirst for God at all. I asked myself, *why is it so hard for me to do the things that were once routine for me, like praying or meditating?* I knew I should be doing these things, but I had no desire to do them. My pain put a wedge between me and God. I knew I needed help to get back on track, so I sought therapy. I explained my lack of spiritual intimacy to my therapist. During one session, she asked me a very challenging question, "What do you believe about God?"

Prior to my diagnosis, I had a very high view of God. He was a close, caring God. He was more than a heavenly being or a savior to me. He was my friend. If you'd asked me in my twenties who God was, I would have rattled off a long list of attributes and shared personal testimonies about how God had blessed my life. Following my diagnosis, my view shifted. My infertility left me questioning things I used to believe.

As followers of Christ, we all have foundational beliefs. We form a view of God based on what we read and hear, but God goes on to reveal Himself to us more intimately through our personal experiences with Him. These personal experiences truly cement our beliefs. Unknowingly, I had allowed my trial to reshape my view of God. He was once a friend I enjoyed spending time with, but now He was a God that felt cold and distant.

This is exactly what the enemy desires: to shake our foundation. But God's character does not depend on our situations. God does not *change*, we do. He is the same God today as He was yesterday, and will be tomorrow. If we believe He is who He says He is, our beliefs must override our external circumstances. Don't allow what you are going through to reshape your image of God. He is almighty God on the mountaintops and He is still almighty God in the valleys.

Meditation: "Let us hold fast the profession of our faith without wavering; (for he is faithful that promised;)." (Hebrews 10:23 KJV)

If you find yourself questioning God in your storm, it's time to reevaluate your core principles and reestablish your foundation. Write down your core beliefs.

.....................................................................................................
.....................................................................................................
.....................................................................................................
.....................................................................................................
.....................................................................................................
.....................................................................................................
.....................................................................................................
.....................................................................................................
.....................................................................................................
.....................................................................................................
.....................................................................................................
.....................................................................................................
.....................................................................................................
.....................................................................................................
.....................................................................................................
.....................................................................................................
.....................................................................................................
.....................................................................................................
.....................................................................................................
.....................................................................................................
.....................................................................................................
.....................................................................................................

# Day 14

## *Root of Bitterness*

"See to it that no one comes short of the grace of God; that no root of bitterness springing up causes trouble, and by it many be defiled." (Hebrews 12:15 New American Standard Bible [NASB])

All my life, I believed in the idea of fairness. I believed that if I lived "right," I deserved a "good life." I would have never admitted this. It only became apparent to me when I was diagnosed, and suddenly I kept thinking how unfair this was. I said to myself, "God, I serve you. I minister, I volunteer. God, I even stayed celibate all those years." It just wasn't fair that I would have to face something so devastating. I was blind to the fact that I became arrogant and prideful, believing that my good behavior should afford me some quid pro quo with God. After all, that would be *fair*. Arrogance turned to bitterness as I wondered, after all I had done, why would God take away something I felt was so precious?

The Bible warns us against bitterness because it is a root that will blossom into a tree (Hebrews 12:15). Sure enough, it had become a fixture in my home, in my life, and in my heart. My world view was shaped by it. It turned my heart away from God and it affected how I interacted with others. I was unhappy and resentful.

Even after I began spending more time with God, I still felt the seeds of bitterness. So how do we deal with bitterness toward God? The first step is to understand that our bitterness is a form of pride and unbelief. We are bitter because something happened that we didn't want to happen, or something didn't happen that we wanted to happen. Humble faith is the only way to overcome bitterness.

We must first humble ourselves. I had to realize that no matter how much "good" I did, I was a sinner and it was only God's grace and mercy that saved me. I didn't deserve anything. Jesus deserved everything, yet he died a painful death on the cross for me because that was God's plan. Everything revolves around God's plan. I had to learn to look at things from a different perspective. It's not about God's plan for *my life*. *My life* is about God's plan. I was created for *His* purpose, not the other way around. Because of God's goodness, I can have faith that I will be blessed along the way, but ultimately it's not all about me.

After humbling ourselves, we must activate our faith. We must learn to trust God when our present reality doesn't meet our expectations. In other words, trust God when life doesn't seem fair. Humble faith says, "God, no matter what I'm facing, Your plan is perfect and my role in Your plan is also perfect."

Meditation: "'For I know the plans I have for you,' declares the Lord, 'plans to prosper you and not to harm you, plans to give you a hope and a future.'" (Jeremiah 29:11 NIV)

Search your heart for roots of bitterness. Confess them and allow humble faith to *change* your present perception.

........................................................................
........................................................................
........................................................................
........................................................................
........................................................................
........................................................................
........................................................................
........................................................................
........................................................................
........................................................................
........................................................................
........................................................................
........................................................................
........................................................................
........................................................................
........................................................................
........................................................................
........................................................................
........................................................................
........................................................................
........................................................................

# Day 15

## *Though He Slay Me*

"Though he slay me, yet will I trust Him." (Job 13:15 NKJV)

The Bible describes Job as an upright and blameless man. Yet we read that suddenly his children died, all his possessions were stripped, and his body became ill. Job's own friends blamed him, believing that surely Job had committed some sin to bring this upon himself. Even his own wife suggested Job "curse God and die" (Job 2:9). What they didn't know was Satan asked God for permission to test Job and God allowed it. Satan wanted to prove a point, that Job only served God because he lacked nothing. Satan believed that if he was allowed to remove all of life's blessings from Job, he would turn his back on God. Sadly, this is exactly what the people closest to Job suggested he do. Through all of his suffering, Job remained faithful to God. He certainly expressed his confusion, frustration, and pain to God, but he refused to turn away from Him.

I encourage you to talk to God sincerely and frequently throughout your situation just as Job did. Job was confused and sought answers from the one He knew could provide them. Talking to God is therapeutic and prevents us from becoming bitter. It's ok to ask God why He has allowed certain things into our lives, but we must be careful that our difficulties do not cause us to question God Himself. In the beginning, I found myself asking God "why me?" But we have to tread carefully so that we do not fall into pride. Pride says "why me," as if we are somehow too good to experience difficulty. Job, however, spoke of his pain but always acknowledged that God is still sovereign. His judgments are right and His ways are perfect.

We must also learn from Job that who we surround ourselves with during difficult times is very important. Even our friends and fellow believers can become a stumbling block for us at times. Surround yourself with those who will pray for you and with you, but let God's voice be the loudest voice in your ear. Spend time in prayer and meditation in order to hear from God. That is what Job did, and in the end he was rewarded with a double portion.

Meditation: "Blessed is the one who perseveres under trial because, having stood the test, that person will receive the crown of life that the Lord has promised to those who love him." (James 1:12 NIV)

Remember that God uses our trials to *change* and conform us into His image. Pray and ask God to speak words of encouragement to you as He molds you.

# Day 16

## *Strength to Endure*

"Not only so, but we also glory in our sufferings, because we know that suffering produces perseverance; perseverance, character; and character, hope." (Romans 5:3–4 NIV)

While I was completing my dermatology residency, I became friends with a surgery resident. No residency is easy, but surgery residencies are particularly labor intense. One night, she was assigned an overnight call on one of the most difficult units. Before she went into work, she asked me to pray for her. She asked me to pray that she would have an easy night. When I got home and set myself to pray, I started to ask for an easy night like she requested, but the Holy Spirit stopped me. Instead, I was prompted to pray a different prayer. Instead of praying for an easy night of work, I prayed that the Lord would give her the strength to endure whatever she encountered. I know you're probably thinking that sounds like a bad friend. Why didn't I just pray for an easy night like she asked? Understand that God uses every circumstance we go through to shape us and equip us. How many valuable learning experiences do we miss simply because we choose the easy way?

We think that praying for ease is the safe prayer, but what is more important than *ease* is that God is with us no matter where we find ourselves.

Take our shepherd David. His job was to watch over the sheep. I'm sure David probably prayed for easy days. "Lord please don't let any sheep stray, and don't let any wild animals eat my flock." No one prays for hard or difficult days at work. That seems absurd. But there's just one problem with ease: It's not the real world. We know that difficult times will come. "In this world you will have trouble," Jesus said (John 16:33 KJV). It's a sure thing. And if David only had easy days, he would never have had the chance to practice his sling-shot by facing lions and bears. Those experiences made him bold and courageous. So when a ten-foot giant roared at the Israelite army, David wasn't afraid. He had been there before. He had faced danger and prevailed. Just as God delivered him out of the mouth of the lion, God would use David to deliver Israel out from under the hand of Goliath.

Meditation: "So do not fear, for I am with you; do not be dismayed, for I am your God. I will strengthen you and help you; I will uphold you with my righteous right hand." (Isaiah 41:10 NIV)

When challenges come, it's human nature to want to pray them away. The training ground called "experience" can be difficult to endure. What we often fail to realize is, those same battles are preparing us, perfecting us, and pushing us toward fulfilling our purpose. Instead of asking God to remove an obstacle, start asking God what He wants you to learn from it. Ask God how He is using your challenges to *change* you, and start *growing* through what you are *going* through.

# Day 17

# *Joy of Contentment*

"I am not saying this because I am in need, for I have learned to be content whatever the circumstances. I know what it is to be in need, and I know what it is to have plenty. I have learned the secret of being content in any and every situation, whether well fed or hungry, whether living in plenty or in want. I can do all this through him who gives me strength." (Philippians 4:11–13 NIV)

Perhaps Paul's greatest strength was found in his contentment. To be in a perpetual state of want is to deny yourself the beauty and blessing of what you already have. The Bible commands us not to covet or yearn for what others have, but it can be difficult seeing others around you receive the blessings you so desperately want or need. When we covet, we make room for envy. James 3:16 (KJV) warns us, "For where envying and strife is, there is confusion and every evil work."

I have struggled in this area as I watch family and friends welcome new life into this world. I am certainly happy for others, but at the same time, I feel the void in my own life. It is much more of a struggle to remain content when what you want isn't "bad," like the desire to be married, have children, restore a relationship, be delivered, healed, or freed from debt. I thought to myself, *God, why can't I have the thing you yourself called "a blessing"?* When we don't get what we want when we want it, we can become discontent. It's impossible to be grateful when we are discontent. This discontent creeps into every area of our life and eventually affects our worship and prayer life. Additionally, when our desires for these things, no matter how good, outweigh our desire for God Himself, it becomes sin. Whatever we exalt above God is an idol and our first command is to put nothing before God. (Exodus 20:3).

Our focus must shift. Our heart's desire should be God Himself, to be godly, and to conform ourselves to the image of Christ. We must first and foremost take pleasure in Him, because after our brief mortal life we spend eternity with Him. The things of this world will no longer matter.

As followers of Christ, we are to "delight ourselves in the Lord" (Psalms 37:4 NKJV). Then the Bible tells us "He will give us the desires of our heart" (Psalms 37:4 NKJV). In other words, instead of focusing on blessings, we must focus on the blesser. When we do, one of two things will happen. God will give us exactly what we desire, *or* His work in us *changes* our desires altogether. Either way, we are blessed.

Meditation: "But godliness with contentment is great gain. For we brought nothing into this world, and it is certain we can carry nothing out." (1 Timothy 6:6 KJV)

Write a list of all the things you do have and thank God with a prayer of gratitude.

# Day 18

# *It's in Your Praise*

"Rejoice in the Lord always; and again I will say, Rejoice!" (Philippians 4:4 NASB)

The Bible tells us to rejoice always, but truthfully, I don't always feel like rejoicing. My grief comes in waves. Sometimes it hits me out of nowhere, while I'm at work, at home watching TV, or at a friend's birthday party. It can be really hard to rejoice when I'm reminded that what I desire so deeply I do not have.

It is difficult to praise when you are hurting or grieving, but this is when you need it most. When we find the strength to profess God's goodness at times when life doesn't feel good, something powerful happens. God's loving arms and His awesome presence rush in and fill our hearts with joy. There's something about praise that lifts us out of our dark places and gives us strength. Praise makes us small, and makes God big. In authentic praise, God becomes so big that our problems suddenly seem small. .

Furthermore, the enemy knows praise and worship are weapons. When God's anointing falls, it has the power to lift burdens and destroy yokes (Isaiah 10:27). In other words, God's anointing can set us free. The devil will work hard to keep us from worshiping. He will distract us, rattle us, and remind us of our trials. We must press on into worship and give God the sacrifice of praise (Hebrews 13:15 KJV). Why would God choose to be somewhere He did not feel welcome? Through praise and worship we can invite God's presence and His anointing into our hearts and our lives.

When I'm overtaken with grief and I can barely get the words out, I just listen and meditate on the lyrics. I allow them to penetrate my heart. Then slowly, I force myself to sing the words over and over again out loud until my heart finds peace and my pain turns to joy. Your praise invites the Holy Spirit to come in and *change* your heart and mind. It's not something to be described, only something to be experienced

Meditation: "...in your presence there is fullness of joy; at your right hand are pleasures forevermore." (Psalm 16:11 ESV)

Write down the lyrics of your favorite song that speak to you the most in this season, then take time to worship.

.............................................................................
.............................................................................
.............................................................................
.............................................................................
.............................................................................
.............................................................................
.............................................................................
.............................................................................
.............................................................................
.............................................................................
.............................................................................
.............................................................................
.............................................................................
.............................................................................
.............................................................................
.............................................................................
.............................................................................
.............................................................................
.............................................................................

# Day 19

## *Who You Say I Am*

"I praise you because I am fearfully and wonderfully made; your works are wonderful, I know that full well." (Psalms 139:14 NIV)

After my diagnosis, I struggled with identity. I would look in the mirror and not recognize myself. Who am I? I was confused, lost, and ashamed. I always saw myself as strong, capable, and...a woman. I believed I walked in the favor and grace of God. But if I was His precious daughter, why would He allow something so devastating to occur? The ability to bear children was central to my idea of womanhood, whether a woman chose to have children or not to have them. But I didn't have that choice. It was taken from me. If my God was so big, so loving, so good, why would He let this happen to me? Since there was obviously nothing wrong with God, subconsciously I began to believe there was something wrong with me. I felt unworthy and I began to question everything I thought I knew about myself.

The enemy kept speaking thoughts of self-doubt and insecurity to me. He loves to use our circumstances to challenge us and our relationship with God. When Jesus went away to fast in the wilderness for forty days, the enemy used this same tactic. Prior to his fasting, Jesus was anointed by God, who stated, "This is my beloved son, in whom I am well pleased" (Matt 3:17 NKJV). After his anointing, Jesus fasted and journeyed through the wilderness. It was there Satan began to tempt Jesus by attacking his identity. Jesus was hungry and tired and Satan knew this. He chose to attack while Jesus was in a vulnerable state. "IF you are the son of God, tell these stones to become bread." Three times Satan challenged Jesus's God-given identity. Similarly, when you are going through trials, Satan will use that opportunity to attack you. You must fight back the way Jesus did, with the word of God. "Jesus answered, 'It is written: "Man shall not live on bread alone, but on every word that comes from the mouth of God""" (Matthew 4:4 NIV). Jesus was sure of his God given identity because he knew the truth of God's word.

When you feel lost and unworthy, remember what God says about you. His word says YOU ARE a royal priesthood. (1 Peter 2:9). YOU ARE the sheep of His pasture. (Ezekiel 34:31). YOU ARE fearfully and wonderfully made. (Psalm 139:14). Hide those words deep in your heart and remember who YOU ARE.

Meditation: "But you are a chosen generation, a royal priesthood, a holy nation, His own special people, that you may proclaim the praises of Him who called you out of darkness into His marvelous light." (1 Peter 2:9 NKJV)

*Change* your mind about YOU. Who does God say that you are?

# Day 20

# *Change of Heart*

When I was a child, I spoke like a child, I thought like a child, I reasoned like a child. When I became a man, I gave up childish ways." (1 Corinthians 13:11 ESV)

When most people think of the heart, they immediately think of emotions, but emotions are only a part of the "heart" as the Bible describes it. The heart we read about in the Bible is composed of three entities: your mind (the decision maker), your will (your effort), and your emotions. Humans will experience a full range of emotions over the course of a lifetime. Your ability to understand, navigate, and control these emotions is pivotal for your growth and maturity. Take an infant or toddler, for example. They respond to everything based on how it makes them "feel." Children do not have the ability to process complex emotions. Feelings such as frustration, confusion, and fear usually result in the same thing, a temper tantrum. To some extent, we excuse mild tantrums because we understand small children are not mature enough to process their emotions. However, after a child reaches a certain age, parents have very little tolerance for tantrums.

Corinthians tells us when we mature in Christ, we are no longer to behave as children. We shouldn't speak, think, and behave like children when we don't get our way or when things are difficult to understand. We should not let emotions lead us like children do. Our emotions can be great motivators, but they are very poor leaders. We often let our emotions lead because that comes naturally to us. When life is stressful, we must be careful not to get too wrapped up in how we feel. Instead, we must rely on what we *know* to be true. This is why studying scripture and hiding God's word in our hearts is vital (Psalm 119:11).

As spirit-filled Christians, we have the ability to discipline ourselves so that we are no longer led by the emotional aspect of the heart. When we hide His word in our hearts (Heart = mind, will, *and* emotions), we face our circumstances like this:

1. We make up our *mind* by relying on the truth of God's word.

2. We *will* ourselves in that direction and put our time and energy into obeying His word.

3. Then, we let our *emotions* follow.

By using this formula, you will find yourself less prone to wild mood swings and tantrums. It is certainly ok to feel strong emotions, but we cannot become consumed by them. If you find yourself in a place where you cannot see past your feelings of anger, disappointment, or pain, start by reminding yourself of God's word. This is beautifully illustrated in Psalms 42. David was in deep anguish because he was being oppressed by his enemies. Throughout the psalm he cries out to God in distress. As the psalm progresses, David begins to recall the goodness of God and questions his own emotions. By the end of the psalm, David has taken control of his emotions and begins to give God praise.

Meditation: "Why are you cast down, O my soul? And why are you disquieted within me? Hope in God; For I shall yet praise Him, The help of my countenance and my God." (Psalm 42:11 NKJV)

*Change* your approach. Practice steps one through three. Reflect on your struggle. Write down the truth of God regarding your situation, will yourself in that direction, then watch as your emotions follow.

......................................................................................

......................................................................................

......................................................................................

......................................................................................

......................................................................................

......................................................................................

......................................................................................

......................................................................................

......................................................................................

......................................................................................

......................................................................................

......................................................................................

......................................................................................

......................................................................................

......................................................................................

......................................................................................

......................................................................................

......................................................................................

## Section Three

# BREAKTHROUGH

"Then you will know the truth, and the truth will set you free."
(John 8:32 NIV)

# Day 21

## *The Small Things*

"Give all your worries and cares to God, for he cares about you." (1 Peter 5:7 NLT)

Why do we as Christians worry when God has already promised to supply all of our needs? For me, it is because I sometimes see God as being concerned about the major things in my life, but indifferent to the small things. Instead of trusting Him with everything, I tend to pray about the BIG things and worry about the little things myself. However, the Bible tells us that God is concerned about every area of our lives. The enemy wants us to believe we cannot go to God with the seemingly small things. He will try to convince us that we are bothering God. Sometimes I fail to go to God, falsely believing that if God wanted something different for my life, He would have made it so.

This way of thinking isn't founded in truth. God cares about *every* detail of our lives. He desires to be intimately involved in our lives. I was reminded of this when I developed a very persistent rash on my face. As a dermatologist, battling a rash for four months without the ability to correctly diagnose or treat myself became extremely frustrating. I tried medicine after medicine to no avail. Finally, I decided to ask for prayer from those in my circle. I'd resisted up to that point because, even though it was a big deal to me, it seemed too insignificant to bring to God. However, within a few days of asking for prayer, God revealed the cause of the rash and I was healed. This was a reminder to me that God cares about EVERY detail of our lives, no matter how small they seem. In fact, the more we allow God to work in our lives, the more faith we build. If we learn to trust God with the small things, we build up our faith for the bigger things. This is how we move from *believing* God to *trusting* God.

Meditation: "Do not be anxious about anything, but in every situation, by prayer and petition, with thanksgiving, present your requests to God. And the peace of God, which transcends all understanding, will guard your hearts and your minds in Christ Jesus." (Philippians 4:6 ESV)

If we can learn to trust God with the small things, we will learn to trust Him for the big things. Write down a prayer for something seemingly small. Remember to come back and write the testimony of your *breakthrough*, detailing how God answered your prayer.

..................................................................................................

..................................................................................................

..................................................................................................

..................................................................................................

..................................................................................................

..................................................................................................

..................................................................................................

..................................................................................................

..................................................................................................

..................................................................................................

..................................................................................................

..................................................................................................

..................................................................................................

..................................................................................................

..................................................................................................

..................................................................................................

..................................................................................................

..................................................................................................

..................................................................................................

..................................................................................................

# Day 22

# *Give Me My Mountain*

"Now therefore, give me this mountain of which the Lord spoke in that day; for you heard in that day how the Anakim were there, and that the cities were great and fortified. It may be that the Lord will be with me, and I shall be able to drive them out as the Lord said. And Joshua blessed him, and gave Hebron to Caleb the son of Jephunneh as an inheritance." (Joshua 14:12–13 NKJV)

Let's revisit the Israelites as they journey to the promised land. After God delivered the Israelites from slavery in Egypt, the Israelites began their journey toward the land God promised them. In the book of Numbers, we meet Caleb, a leader from the tribe of Judah. Caleb and eleven other leaders were sent to spy on the land of Canaan, the place where the Israelites would later settle. The Israelite spies found their way to Hebron, a city perched at the top of a mountain. After forty days, the spies returned to Moses and Aaron and gave their report. They describe the land as "flowing with milk and honey." In other words, the land was lush and desirable. However, ten of the spies became so frightened by the giants inhabiting the land that they began to spread fear among the camp.

Only two of the spies had anything positive to say. Caleb tells them, "Let us go up at once and take possession, for we are well able to overcome it." He and Joshua describe the land as "exceedingly good" (Numbers 14:7). Caleb warns them not to "rebel against the Lord" and to not "be afraid of the people of the land" (Numbers 14:9). Unfortunately, the report of the ten spies caused so much doubt and uncertainty that the Israelites were too afraid to move forward into Canaan. God was so angry that He declared none of the Israelites in that generation would ever see the promised land except Caleb and Joshua. God was so pleased with Caleb's faith that God promised the most desirable city, Hebron, to Caleb.

After various battles, the Israelites did eventually conquer Canaan. Forty-five years later, Joshua succeeded Moses as the leader of the Israelites. Caleb approached Joshua and demanded what God promised him, the city of Hebron. Joshua, under God's direction, gives Caleb the city of Hebron "because he wholly followed the Lord God of Israel" (Joshua 14:14). God promised Caleb Hebron. Caleb, exercising his faith, simply asked God for what was rightfully his. Caleb's faith and insistence were rewarded.

Meditation: "God is not a man, that he should lie; neither the son of man, that he should repent: hath he said, and shall he not do it? or hath he spoken, and shall he not make it good?" (Numbers 23:19 NKJV)

God is faithful and if He has spoken a promise to you, He must deliver. Despite what you are going through or how long it has been, God is bound by His word. Think back to what God has spoken to you and over you. Bring those God-given dreams, visions, and promises back to the forefront of your mind. Remind God of His promises and confess your faith that He will bring it to pass. Your *breakthrough* is coming.

# SECTION THREE: **BREAKTHROUGH**

# Day 23

## *Wait for It*

"God also said to Abraham, 'As for Sarai your wife, you are no longer to call her Sarai; her name will be Sarah. I will bless her and will surely give you a son by her. I will bless her so that she will be the mother of nations; kings of peoples will come from her.' Abraham fell facedown; he laughed and said to himself, 'Will a son be born to a man a hundred years old? Will Sarah bear a child at the age of ninety?'" (Genesis 17:15–17 NIV)

There are two words for time in the Greek language: *chronos* and *kairos*. Chronos refers to a calendar date or specific time. Kairos means the right time, or opportune time. God promised Abraham and Sarah a child in their old age. This child was to be born in God's appointed time. However, to their dismay, God's "kairos" did not fit their "chronos." As a result of impatience, Abraham conceived a child with the handmaiden Hagar. This is not what God intended, and this decision to force God's timing resulted in much turmoil. Sarah became so jealous of Hagar she ultimately had her and the child sent away.

The Israelites made the same mistake. When the Israelites became impatient with the judges God appointed over them, they demanded God send them a king (1 Samuel 8:5 NKJV). It was not the request that dishonored God. Instead, it was the Israelites' rejection of God and His perfect plan and perfect timing. The Israelites desired to be like other nations more than they desired God's will. God granted their request but warned them what kind of king they would get. Saul was mighty in battle, just like the Israelites desired, but his heart was far from God. What could Israel have avoided if they were willing to wait a little longer for David, a man after God's own heart? David brought them victory in battle and brought them under the obedience of God.

Like Abraham, Sarah, and the Israelites, there were many times when I was tempted to try and "fix" my situation on my own. God had given me clear instructions to trust in Him. He told me that what He was going to do was outside of logic, outside of science, but still, I struggled with the idea that perhaps I could help God and move things along. I desired what I wanted more than I desired God's will to be done in my life.

On your faith journey, you are going to be tempted by impatience. You will be tempted because others have what you desire. You will be presented with opportunities to do it your way. God might even allow it. But never mistake His permission for His blessing. Trusting God completely requires you to put your full weight on Him. No backup plan, no contingency, no other options. It's scary, I know. God is searching for those who trust Him wholeheartedly, because your miracle will bring Him the ultimate glory. Do not rob God of His glory. Do not rob yourself of His perfect blessing. God has a perfect plan, and when it's time, He will make it happen. Lord, teach us to wait on you. It's worth it.

Meditation: "Wait on the LORD: be of good courage, and he shall strengthen your heart: wait, I say, on the LORD." (Psalms 27:14 NKJV)

Are you growing impatient because you have not received your breakthrough? Write a prayer to guard your heart against impatience.

# Day 24

## *Temporary Pain*

"For this light momentary affliction is preparing for us an eternal weight of glory beyond all comparison, as we look not to the things that are seen but to the things that are unseen. For the things that are seen are transient, but the things that are unseen are eternal." (2 Corinthians 4:17-18 ESV)

When we are in the midst of a trial, there is a tendency to become shortsighted. It's difficult to see beyond our present circumstances. I couldn't see a life without pain or the emptiness of not being able to bear my own children. I often found myself wondering if I would always feel like this. Would I always feel this bad? Would I always feel this empty?

You may be feeling similarly. The pain of what you are going through right now is so overwhelming, you can't see a way through it or imagine a life without it. Despite how you feel right now, there will come a day when it will sting a little less. The weight will be a little lighter. The heartbreak will heal. You will smile again. You will laugh and experience real joy. When I find myself slipping back into despair, I tell myself, "I won't always feel like this." It allows me to acknowledge my present struggle, while still giving myself hope for the future. Even more, as children of God, we have assurance that our current struggles are preparing us for what is to come. They are growing us in uncomfortable but necessary ways. We have to trust that our present struggles have an eternal purpose. Even though we don't see it right now, here's a sneak peek: It's going to be good!

I don't know if it's tomorrow, or the day after, or next month, or next year, but there will be a day when morning comes and night will be a memory. Keep looking ahead and hang on until morning.

Meditation: "...weeping may stay for the night, but rejoicing comes in the morning." (Psalms 30:5 NIV)

Paint a picture of yourself healed and whole. Picture your *breakthrough*.

........................................................................................

........................................................................................

........................................................................................

........................................................................................

........................................................................................

........................................................................................

........................................................................................

........................................................................................

........................................................................................

........................................................................................

........................................................................................

........................................................................................

........................................................................................

........................................................................................

........................................................................................

........................................................................................

........................................................................................

........................................................................................

........................................................................................

# Day 25

## *For My Good*

"But as for you, you meant evil against me; but God meant it for good, in order to bring it about as it is this day, to save many people alive." (Genesis 50:20 NKJV)

It is very hard to see the good in a bad situation. Hearing the words "you will never have biological children" felt like taking a bullet. In those overwhelming moments it can be extremely hard to focus on anything except our present circumstances. I certainly wasn't thinking about ministry or service. However, no matter how bad things get, or how narrow our view becomes, we have to remember that God sees the full picture. Scripture tells us the Lord is the alpha and omega (Revelation 1:8 NKJV) and He knows the beginning and sees all the way to the end (Isaiah 46:10 NKJV). God's plan sometimes includes trials that we may not understand until the end is revealed.

Joseph provides a great example. Joseph was thrown into a pit by his jealous brothers, sold into slavery, falsely accused, and imprisoned. I'm sure none of that felt good. Despite his situation going from bad to worse, Joseph was faithful to God and waited on

Him for deliverance. Joseph may have wondered or asked God why such horrible things happened to him, but Joseph never turned away from God. Joseph stayed faithful and even allowed his gifts to be used while unlawfully imprisoned. It was in the prison that Joseph was able to use his gift of interpreting dreams. Exercising that gift eventually granted him an audience with the king. In the end, Joseph was able to save not only his own family but an entire nation from famine. The narrative of Joseph demonstrates two important principles. First, that God's purposes will ultimately prevail. Second, God doesn't just deliver us from bad situations; He can use those very circumstances to bring us to a place of victory, bless those around us, and bring Him glory.

It's easy to see how God is working for us when things are going well. It's hard to see His goodness amid our trials. But no matter how it feels, we must rely on the truth of who God is. He is our good father. He desires good for us and promised to not withhold anything good from those who walk uprightly (Psalms 84:11 NKJV). These *breakthroughs* and blessings come in God's perfect time when we remain faithful. Grief and pain can cause us to focus on ourselves and ignore our calling and spiritual gifts. We must allow God to use us even during our trials because you never know how, when, or where God might show up to change our situations.

Meditation: "And we know that all things work together for good to those who love God, to those who are the called according to His purpose." (Romans 8:28 NKJV)

Reflect on your spiritual gifts. Ask God to give you the strength and courage to use them during this season. They just might be the key to your *breakthrough*.

# Day 26

# *When God Says No*

"And I pleaded with the Lord at that time, saying, 'O Lord God, you have only begun to show your servant your greatness and your mighty hand. For what god is there in heaven or on earth who can do such works and mighty acts as yours? Please let me go over and see the good land beyond the Jordan, that good hill country and Lebanon.' But the Lord was angry with me because of you and would not listen to me. And the Lord said to me, 'Enough from you; do not speak to me of this matter again. Go up to the top of Pisgah and lift up your eyes westward and northward and southward and eastward, and look at it with your eyes, for you shall not go over this Jordan.'" (Deuteronomy 3:23–27 ESV)

Moses was chosen by God to lead the Israelites out of captivity and into the promised land. During the journey, Moses not only faced opposition from foreign nations but from within his own camp. In Numbers 20, the Israelites complained to Moses and Aaron that they had no water. God gave Moses instructions to speak to the rock and water would come forth. Instead of speaking to the rock, Moses, out of anger, took his staff and struck the rock twice.

SECTION THREE: **BREAKTHROUGH**

Because of his disobedience, Moses was not allowed to enter the promised land. In Deuteronomy Chapter 3, we see Moses ask God to reconsider his punishment, but God says no. Moses, a prophet, a leader, a patriarch of faith who spoke with God face to face (Exodus 33:11), was told no. If God said no to Moses, after all he'd endured, then we must understand, sometimes He will say no to us as well.

Many scholars go to great depths to explain why Moses's actions led to such a harsh punishment. What we as followers of Christ need to understand is that no matter who we are, or what good things we have done, no one is above God's law. Sometimes our own actions or inactions may lead us into difficult circumstances. This does not mean that every challenge or disappointment we face is our fault, but we do have to accept responsibility and repent when necessary. Even then, we must not expect that God will remove the consequences of our actions. However, because of His love for us, God's grace will always restore us. We see this act of grace when God allows Moses to lay eyes on the promised land, and later when Moses appears at the transfiguration of Jesus (Matthew 17:3). Although Moses did not get what he asked for, he received something far greater. We can expect that God will also do the same for us when we repent.

Meditation: "After you have suffered a little while, the God of all grace, who has called you to his eternal glory in Christ, will himself restore, confirm, strengthen, and establish you." (1 Peter 5:10 ESV)

Don't let unconfessed sin keep you from your *breakthrough*. Ask the Holy Spirit to reveal any unconfessed sin. Pray a prayer of confession. Repent and ask God to restore you.

...........................................................................

...........................................................................

...........................................................................

...........................................................................

...........................................................................

...........................................................................

...........................................................................

...........................................................................

...........................................................................

...........................................................................

...........................................................................

...........................................................................

...........................................................................

...........................................................................

...........................................................................

...........................................................................

...........................................................................

...........................................................................

...........................................................................

...........................................................................

...........................................................................

...........................................................................

...........................................................................

...........................................................................

...........................................................................

...........................................................................

# Day 27

## *Even If*

"Shadrach, Meshach, and Abed-Nego answered and said to the king, 'O Nebuchadnezzar, we have no need to answer you in this matter. If that is the case, our God whom we serve is able to deliver us from the burning fiery furnace, and He will deliver us from your hand, O king. But if not, let it be known to you, O king, that we do not serve your gods, nor will we worship the gold image which you have set up.'" (Daniel 3:16–18 NKJV)

The three Hebrew boys were sentenced to death because they refused to bow down and worship the statue of Nebuchadnezzar. They refused to break the first commandment and worship a graven image. The Hebrew boys knew the consequences of their refusal, but their holy fear of God would not allow them to yield.

While many of us are not facing a literal fiery furnace, our trials can and will test our faith. There may be times when we are tempted to bow physically or spiritually. We will be tempted to take the easy way out or give up all together. But our response as true believers must resemble Shadrach, Meshach, and Abed-Nego. We must remain faithful to God

Responding in faith accomplishes three things. First, it compels God to act. Nothing moves God as much as our faith. Matthew 17:20 says, "if you have faith like a grain of mustard seed, you will say to this mountain, 'Move from here to there,' and it will move, and nothing will be impossible for you" (ESV). Secondly, it strengthens us. After being bound and placed in the furnace, Nebuchadnezzar saw Shadrach, Meshach, and Abed-Nego walking unbound in the furnace. Our faith in God allows us to walk freely in the midst of our trials when others expect that we should be consumed by them. Lastly, responding in faith can be a testimony to those around us. When the three Hebrew boys emerged unscathed from the fire, Nebuchadnezzar's response was to recognize the power and authority of the God they served. Now that's a *breakthrough*!

Meditation: "But He knoweth the way that I take; when He hath tried me, I shall come forth as gold." (Job 23:10 KJV)

In what ways are you tempted to bow? Confess them and ask God to strengthen your resolve so that you may be an example to those around you..

......................................................................................................
......................................................................................................
......................................................................................................
......................................................................................................
......................................................................................................
......................................................................................................
......................................................................................................
......................................................................................................
......................................................................................................
......................................................................................................
......................................................................................................
......................................................................................................
......................................................................................................
......................................................................................................
......................................................................................................
......................................................................................................
......................................................................................................
......................................................................................................
......................................................................................................
......................................................................................................
......................................................................................................

# Day 28

# *Nevertheless*

"Father, if you are willing, remove this cup from me. Nevertheless, not my will, but yours, be done." (Luke 22:42 ESV)

From the time Jesus came of age and began his ministry, he was fully aware of how his story would end. No matter how many miracles he performed, no matter how many people followed him in the crowd, he would still face crucifixion. Jesus knew these things years before they occurred, yet when he was moments away from being captured, he was overwhelmed with anguish. He prayed to God and asked if there was another way.

I love this moment in the gospel because it shows Jesus's humanity. Much of the gospel is devoted to showing that Jesus was the son of God, but these verses show that Jesus, just like you and me, found himself in circumstances that were too much for him to bear alone. Jesus did not want to go to the cross, but He understood that his desires came second to God's will. He recited what I believe is the most powerful but difficult of prayers. "Nevertheless, not my will, but yours be done" (Luke 22:42 ESV). Jesus could have evaded capture, ran, or fought back. He could have called down the powers of heaven and destroyed everyone that plotted against him. However, that was not God's will. Jesus knew God had a plan and it included his pain and suffering. So instead of fighting against God's will, Jesus surrendered to it.

When we find ourselves in a situation we do not want to be in, we must first pray and seek God's wisdom. Sometimes our sin and disobedience lead us into difficult circumstances. If that is the case, we have to repent. Other times, when God has allowed us to fall into trials, we may not understand how our pain is part of God's plan. No matter what, our response should be like that of Jesus. Crucify your will and get in alignment with God. The Bible says shortly after Jesus submitted to God's will, an angel appeared and strengthened him (Luke 22:43). God will also strengthen us.

Meditation: "I have been crucified with Christ and I no longer live, but Christ lives in me. The life I now live in the body, I live by faith in the Son of God, who loved me and gave himself for me." (Galatians 2:20 ESV)

Make a choice today to adopt a nevertheless attitude. Your *breakthrough* is on the other side of obedience. Write out your own prayer of submission.

# Day 29

# *It Is Finished*

"His parents went to Jerusalem every year at the Feast of the Passover. And when He was twelve years old, they went up to Jerusalem according to the custom of the feast. When they had finished the days, as they returned, the Boy Jesus lingered behind in Jerusalem. And Joseph and His mother did not know it; but supposing Him to have been in the company, they went a day's journey, and sought Him among their relatives and acquaintances. So when they did not find Him, they returned to Jerusalem, seeking Him. Now so it was that after three days they found Him in the temple, sitting in the midst of the teachers, both listening to them and asking them questions. And all who heard Him were astonished at His understanding and answers. So when they saw Him, they were amazed; and His mother said to Him, 'Son, why have You done this to us? Look, Your father and I have sought You anxiously.' And He said to them, 'Why did you seek Me? Did you not know that I must be about My Father's business?'" (Luke 2:41–49 NKJV)

Our lives here on earth are short. The Bible describes our time here as a "vapor" (James 4:14 NKJV). Even from a young age, Jesus understood that time was of the essence. Chronologically, the first recorded words of Jesus were, "Did you not know that I must be about my father's business?" (Luke 2:49 NKJV) God had a purpose and a plan when He sent His only begotten son to earth. Much like Jesus, God has a calling on our lives. Not one of us has been left out of God's plan. God is working diligently to bring His plans for us to completion (Philippians 1:6).

Every one of us was born into this world on purpose, with purpose, for a purpose. Much can be accomplished in this short time when we are focused on our Father's business. There were many distractions that could have derailed Jesus. He wisely chose to focus on his mission. Isaiah 53:3 NIV says, "He was despised and rejected by mankind, a man of suffering, and familiar with pain. Like one from whom people hide their faces he was despised, and we held him in low esteem." If anyone had an excuse to give up, it was Jesus. Throughout his entire life, he was called a liar, he was mocked, and he was falsely accused. God's ultimate purpose prevailed, and Jesus ended his life here on earth with these words: "It is finished" (John 19:30 NIV). Jesus was able to accomplish everything God had planned for him. When your time comes, will you be able to say, *I have fought the good fight, I have finished the race, I have kept the faith* (2 Timothy 4:7 NIV), or will you use your difficult circumstances as your excuse?

Despite his trials, betrayal, and physical suffering, Jesus accomplished His mission. He was able to persevere because God's very spirit lived inside of him. Likewise, we cannot accomplish God's will on our own. Jesus knew we would need a guiding presence, so He placed in us the Holy Spirit.

Meditation: "And I will ask the Father, and He will give you another Helper (Comforter, Advocate, Intercessor—Counselor, Strengthener, Standby), to be with you forever." (John 14:16 Amplified Bible, Classic Edition [AMPC])

Pray and ask God to fill you with His Holy Spirit and give you the supernatural ability to keep pressing toward God's purpose and your *breakthrough.*

...........................................................................................
...........................................................................................
...........................................................................................
...........................................................................................
...........................................................................................
...........................................................................................
...........................................................................................
...........................................................................................
...........................................................................................
...........................................................................................
...........................................................................................
...........................................................................................
...........................................................................................
...........................................................................................
...........................................................................................
...........................................................................................
...........................................................................................
...........................................................................................
...........................................................................................

# Day 30

# *Recommissioned*

"Therefore go and make disciples of all nations, baptizing them in the name of the Father and of the Son and of the Holy Spirit, and teaching them to obey everything I have commanded you. And surely I am with you always, to the very end of the age." (Matthew 28:19–20 NIV)

Despite all the miracles Jesus performed in the presence of the disciples, Jesus's crucifixion seemed so final. Despite the prophecies and promises that Jesus would return, the disciples could not see past a body wrapped and buried in a tomb. Jesus's death felt like the end so the disciples scattered and returned to their previous lives.

After the resurrection Jesus sought his disciples, but he did not find them waiting at the tomb, preaching to the gentiles or healing the sick. Instead, Jesus found Peter doing the very job he was called out of, *fishing*. Peter, likely embarrassed by his denial of Jesus and paralyzed by the crucifixion, forgot his purpose. In Matthew Chapter 16, Jesus prophesied over Peter, saying, "You are Peter, and on this rock I will build my church, and the gates of hell shall not prevail against it" (Matthew 16:18 NIV). Stricken with grief, Peter abandoned his assignment. To set things right, Jesus went in search of Peter and recommissioned him. Jesus's instructions to Peter: "Feed my sheep" (John 21:17 NIV). In other words, get back on track!

Grief, pain, and guilt may cause us to abandon God's mission. Instead of allowing God to take care of us, we feel the need to take care of ourselves, and often this leads to abandoning God's purpose and God's people. However, we must remember God has called us out of our previous lives and into new life with Him. We cannot let trials cause us to go backward. Instead of letting our difficulties hold us back, allow them to push us forward into God's plan for our lives. A life full of purpose will bring joy to even the darkest of circumstances.

Meditation: "For we are God's handiwork, created in Christ Jesus to do good works, which God prepared in advance for us to do." (Ephesians 2:10 NIV)

Ask God to renew your sense of purpose. Walking in your true purpose is the path to your *breakthrough*.

...........................................................................................

...........................................................................................

...........................................................................................

...........................................................................................

...........................................................................................

...........................................................................................

...........................................................................................

...........................................................................................

...........................................................................................

...........................................................................................

...........................................................................................

...........................................................................................

...........................................................................................

...........................................................................................

...........................................................................................

...........................................................................................

...........................................................................................

...........................................................................................

...........................................................................................

...........................................................................................

...........................................................................................

# Not the end...

I pray you have been blessed over the past thirty days. Moreover, I pray this is not the end but only the beginning of a new season of fresh anointing for you. I speak the name of Jesus over you. I speak peace to your situation. I speak healing, reconciliation, and restoration. I speak forgiveness, grace, and favor over your life. I speak financial provision and career breakthroughs over you. I pray against fear, doubt, and confusion. I pray against depression, loneliness, and isolation. I pray the God of wonders reveals Himself in new ways to you and that you fall more and more in love with Jesus every day. Now breakthrough.

Made in the USA
Middletown, DE
15 December 2023

45801094R00066